TAMPA BAY RAYS

BY LUKE HANLON

SportsZone

An Imprint of Abdo Publishing
abdobooks.com

abdobooks.com

Published by Abdo Publishing, a division of ABDO, PO Box 398166, Minneapolis, Minnesota 55439. Copyright © 2023 by Abdo Consulting Group, Inc. International copyrights reserved in all countries. No part of this book may be reproduced in any form without written permission from the publisher. SportsZone™ is a trademark and logo of Abdo Publishing.

Printed in the United States of America, North Mankato, Minnesota.
102022
012023

Cover Photo: Jim McIsaac/Getty Images Sport/Getty Images
Interior Photos: Ezra Shaw/Getty Images Sport/Getty Images, 4, 6, 36; Doug Collier/AFP/Getty Images, 9; Larry Goren/Four Seam Images/AP Images, 11; Andy Lyons/Getty Images Sport/Getty Images, 12; John Williamson/Major League Baseball/Getty Images, 14; Al Behrman/AP Images, 16; Michael Dwyer/AP Images, 19; Mike Carlson/AP Images, 20, 31; Mark Humphrey/AP Images, 22; Phelan M. Ebenhack/AP Images, 24; Chris O'Meara/AP Images, 27, 28; Jim McIsaac/Getty Images Sport/Getty Images, 32; Jae C. Hong/AP Images, 38; Michael Reaves/Getty Images Sport/Getty Images, 39; Randy Litzinger/Icon Sportswire/AP Images, 41

Editor: Charlie Beattie
Series Designer: Becky Daum

Library of Congress Control Number: 2022940490

Publisher's Cataloging-in-Publication Data

Names: Hanlon, Luke, author.
Title: Tampa Bay Rays / by Luke Hanlon
Description: Minneapolis, Minnesota: Abdo Publishing, 2023 | Series: Inside MLB |
    Includes online resources and index.
Identifiers: ISBN 9781098290344 (lib. bdg.) | ISBN 9781098275549 (ebook)
Subjects: LCSH: Tampa Bay Rays (Baseball team)--Juvenile literature. | Baseball
    teams--Juvenile literature. | Professional sports--Juvenile literature. | Sports
    franchises--Juvenile literature. | Major League Baseball (Organization)--Juvenile
    literature.
Classification: DDC 796.35764--dc23

TABLE OF

CONTENTS

CHAPTER 1

BAY BEGINNINGS 4

CHAPTER 2

RAY OF SUN 12

CHAPTER 3

BETTER LATE THAN NEVER ..24

CHAPTER 4

CASHING IN 32

TIMELINE 42

TEAM FACTS 44

TEAM TRIVIA 45

GLOSSARY 46

MORE INFORMATION 47

ONLINE RESOURCES 47

INDEX 48

ABOUT THE AUTHOR 48

BAY BEGINNINGS

On October 17, 2020, the Tampa Bay Rays were one game away from the team's second World Series appearance. All that stood between the team and a title chance was a win in Game 7 of the American League Championship Series (ALCS). Playing in this Game 7 was not something to celebrate, though. In the best-of-seven series, the Rays had won the first three games. The Houston Astros battled back to tie it up. Only once in Major League Baseball (MLB) history had a team ever lost a series after being up 3–0. The fate of both teams' seasons came down to one game.

The Astros were playing in their fourth straight ALCS. They had played in Game 7s before. The Rays were far less

Randy Arozarena connects on his two-run homer against the Houston Astros in Game 7 of the 2020 ALCS.

Arozarena tosses away his batting helmet rounding first base as teammates celebrate behind him.

experienced and needed an early spark to calm their nerves. They got one when right fielder Manuel Margot was hit by the first pitch in the bottom of the first inning. Two batters later, Randy Arozarena stepped to the plate. The rookie outfielder had made his debut for the Rays on August 30 of that year. He had been hot ever since. Arozarena tallied 18 hits and seven home runs in 23 regular-season games. He was even better in the playoffs. Arozarena had 20 hits and six home runs in 13 postseason games heading into Game 7. Now he had a chance to come through in the biggest game of his life.

On the mound for Houston was veteran righty Lance
McCullers Jr. That didn't faze Arozarena. He worked the
count to 2–2. Then he got the pitch he was looking for and
slammed it toward the right-center-field wall. Arozarena knew
it was gone as soon as he left the batter's box. He let out a
scream toward the Tampa Bay bench in celebration. As he
rounded first base, he tossed his bat away. His helmet also
came flying off. Arozarena had put his team up 2–0 with his
seventh postseason home run. That broke a rookie record
held by former Rays star Evan Longoria. And it gave the Rays a
much-needed confidence boost in a must-win game.

IF YOU BUILD IT, THEY WILL COME

The Tampa/St. Petersburg area of Florida has a long history
with America's pastime. The St. Petersburg Saints started
playing as a semipro team in 1908. Six years later, the
St. Louis Browns became the first major league team to
use St. Petersburg as a spring training home. Spring training
remains a tradition in the Tampa–St. Petersburg area today.
But it took decades for the area to get its own MLB team.

In 1976 Tampa got its first major professional sports
team when the Buccaneers debuted in the National Football
League. Once the area got one team, it clamored for more.
St. Petersburg Times columnist Jack Lake started writing

regularly about bringing a professional baseball team to St. Petersburg. Lake's work helped inspire local businessmen to form the Tampa Bay Baseball Group (TBBG) in 1983.

The TBBG's efforts mostly focused on trying to get existing teams to move to Florida. Anytime an MLB team was struggling to build a new stadium, the TBBG offered some money to bring the team to Tampa. But this plan never worked. Usually teams used Tampa's offer to pressure their current cities into a new stadium deal. So the group tried a different idea in 1985. They received $85 million from the city of St. Petersburg to build a stadium that might attract a team. The Florida Suncoast Dome opened five years later.

It took five more years, but in 1995, MLB finally granted the city's wish. By then local businessman Vince Naimoli was in charge of the TBBG. When MLB granted two new teams, Naimoli became the owner of the new Tampa franchise. The team was set up to start playing in 1998.

GEOGRAPHY LESSON

Tampa Bay is home to three professional sports teams, but Tampa Bay is not an actual city. Tampa Bay refers to the metro area that consists of the city of Tampa, along with St. Petersburg, Clearwater, and four surrounding counties. While the Buccaneers and Lightning play in the city of Tampa, the Rays play in St. Petersburg.

Vince Naimoli poses with the Rays' original uniform at a press conference in 1995.

Naimoli wanted to name the team the Sting Rays. But that name was already being used by a minor league team in Hawaii. So Naimoli went with Devil Rays after the type of rays found in the waters of Tampa Bay.

GROWING PAINS

The Devil Rays and Arizona Diamondbacks built their first rosters through an expansion draft in 1997. The other MLB teams could protect 15 players from their rosters. Anyone who wasn't protected could be taken by the new teams. The Devil Rays took pitcher Tony Saunders from the Florida Marlins with

HOMETOWN HEROES

One thing the Devil Rays did consistently in their early years was to sign players who grew up in the Tampa Bay area. Both Wade Boggs and Fred McGriff played high school baseball in Tampa. The Devil Rays went on to acquire other local veterans like pitcher Dwight Gooden in 2000 and Tino Martinez in 2004. Martinez and McGriff grew up playing together, and both attended Jefferson High School four years apart.

the top pick in the draft, hoping he could be a star pitcher. It didn't work out. Saunders appeared in only 40 games for Tampa Bay. In 1998 he led the league with 111 walks. The Devil Rays were on to something with their third pick, which they used to take promising outfielder Bobby Abreu. But he never played for Tampa Bay at all. The Devil Rays traded him to the Philadelphia Phillies for infielder Kevin Stocker. Abreu went on to two All-Star Games and was a consistently good player for more than a decade. The Devil Rays released Stocker in 2000.

Despite those poor decisions, Tampa Bay fans were excited for baseball. Opening Day tickets sold out in 17 minutes. The Devil Rays played their first game on March 31, 1998. They hosted the Detroit Tigers in St. Petersburg's domed stadium, now named Tropicana Field. The Tigers won 11–6. The Devil Rays got their first win the next night, beating Detroit 11–8.

That first win led to a hot start. Veteran stars like third baseman Wade Boggs and first baseman Fred McGriff helped

Fred McGriff led the Devil Rays with 19 home runs and 81 runs batted in (RBIs) during the team's inaugural 1998 season.

Tampa Bay compete with the established teams. The Devil Rays had a 10–6 record after 16 games. That was the first time an expansion team had ever been four games over .500 in its first season. But it didn't last. The team finished with a 63–99 record, last in the American League (AL) East.

CHAPTER 2

RAY OF SUN

The Devil Rays won six more games in 1999 than the year before, but they still finished in last place. The season's biggest highlight came from Wade Boggs. The veteran star collected his 3,000th career hit on August 7 against Cleveland. Boggs was the first player in MLB history whose 3,000th hit was a home run.

Still, the team was not in a good place. Baseball teams have two main ways to build their rosters. One is through free agency. The other is by drafting and developing amateur players. Tampa Bay had started drafting in 1996, two years before its first game. But none of the team's first three drafts produced much. So after two losing seasons, team owner Vince

Wade Boggs acknowledges the crowd after collecting his 3,000th hit on August 7, 1999.

Carl Crawford led the AL in triples four times in nine seasons with the Rays, including a career-high 19 in 2004.

Naimoli decided to lean on free agency and add more veterans in 2000.

Naimoli spent more than $62 million on the team's roster. A big part of that went to slugging outfielder Greg Vaughn. He led the team in home runs that year. In 2001 he did it again while also making the All-Star Game. But most of Naimoli's other signings did not work out. And the Devil Rays finished last each year.

Some of the team's draft struggles were the result of bad luck. In 1999 the Devil Rays had the top pick and selected Josh Hamilton. The young outfielder was considered a sure star. But off-field problems meant Hamilton never played for the Devil Rays. He eventually reached the majors. Hamilton even won the AL Most Valuable Player (MVP) Award in 2010. But none of that happened in Tampa.

THE ROOKIE

Jim Morris had played minor-league baseball for parts of five seasons in the 1980s. But arm injuries forced him to retire in 1989. A decade later, he was coaching high school baseball in Big Lake, Texas. He made a deal with his players that if they won the district championship, he would try out for a major league team. The players came through, so Morris tried out for the Devil Rays. He threw 98 miles per hour at the tryout and earned a new minor-league contract. In September 1999, Tampa Bay called the now 35-year-old Morris up to the majors. His story was later made in to the 2002 film *The Rookie*.

Andrew Friedman, *left,* and Joe Maddon, *right,* helped lead the Rays to their first winning season in 2008.

In 2000 the Devil Rays selected Rocco Baldelli. The center fielder reached the majors in 2003 and was third in AL Rookie of the Year voting. Writers compared the young star to legendary New York Yankee Joe DiMaggio. But Baldelli soon struggled with injuries. He was never able to build on his rookie season.

Things finally began looking up with Carl Crawford. After the Devil Rays picked him in the second round in 1999, the speedy outfielder made his major league debut in 2002 and became the team's first homegrown star. Many more were right behind him, as Tampa Bay started to find better talent through the draft in the early 2000s. But even Crawford's potential didn't help the Devil Rays in 2002. The team finished 55–106, the worst record in its short history.

With the losing seasons piling up, fans lost interest quickly. Attendance at games fell every year from Tampa's first season through 2003. That same year Tampa native Lou Piniella debuted as the team's new manager. "Sweet Lou" was known for his fiery temper. He had won a World Series managing the Cincinnati Reds in 1990. However, Piniella didn't have that same success in Tampa Bay. He stepped down after another last-place finish in 2005.

NO MORE DEVIL

Three new figures soon turned the team around. Investor Stuart Sternberg bought the Devil Rays from Naimoli in October 2005. Once Sternberg bought the team, he promoted

29-year-old Andrew Friedman to be the general manager. The young executive wanted to use a different approach to allow the low-budget Devil Rays a chance to compete with big-spending division rivals like the Yankees and the Boston Red Sox. Friedman started using analytics to unearth a new group of young players for Tampa Bay.

He also hired another new face to lead the team on the field. Joe Maddon had only 51 games of managing experience when he was hired. But he was taking over a team with lots of young talent. Crawford was already an All-Star. Starting pitcher Scott Kazmir made his first All-Star team in 2006 as a 22-year-old. Talented outfield prospects B. J. Upton and Delmon Young started to play consistently in 2006 as well.

Maddon knew he couldn't completely turn the team around right away. Even with new ownership, the Devil Rays struggled on the field. Tampa Bay finished last in the AL East in each of Maddon's first two seasons in charge.

Sternberg also made one more big change off the field. He had wanted to change the name of the team since he became the owner. Sternberg wanted to change the team's image after a decade of poor performances. Fans had also been asking to remove *Devil* from the team's name for years. After the 2007 season, Sternberg dropped *Devil* and renamed the team the Tampa Bay Rays. The team also changed its uniform design

Scott Kazmir, wearing the Rays new-look uniforms, fires a pitch against the Boston Red Sox in 2008.

and colors. The original logo of a Devil Ray was replaced by a sunburst.

Even with the new name and look, the team started slowly in 2008. The Rays were just 11–11 on April 25. That day they took on the Boston Red Sox. In one of only 47 plate appearances he had that season, designated hitter Nathan Haynes hit a walk-off single to score Crawford and win the game.

Evan Longoria was an All-Star in each of his first three MLB seasons.

Tampa Bay did not fall below .500 at any point for the rest of the season.

A few stars emerged in 2008. None were bigger than third baseman Evan Longoria. The Rays had taken Longoria third overall in the 2006 draft. He didn't make the 2008 roster out of spring training. But he got the call up two weeks into the season and never looked back. The sweet-swinging Longoria led the team in slugging percentage. Only first baseman Carlos Peña had more home runs and RBIs. Longoria made the All-Star team and won the AL Rookie of the Year.

OCTOBER BASEBALL

The Rays finished the 2008 season 97–65. They were only the ninth team ever to win their division a season after finishing in last place. The incredible turnaround was 31 wins better than the year before.

In their first postseason series, the Rays took care of the Chicago White Sox 3–1 in the AL Division Series (ALDS). The defending World Series champions, the Red Sox, were up next in the ALCS. Boston won Game 1 in Tampa Bay. Game 2 went to extra innings tied 8–8. But just as they had done against Boston in April, the Rays won in walk-off fashion. Upton hit a sacrifice fly to right field in the 11th to score Fernando Perez and even the series.

Rays catcher Dioner Navarro, *right,* celebrates with rookie pitcher David Price after the final out of the 2008 ALCS.

That win sparked the Rays. They won the next two games in Boston by a combined score of 22–5. Longoria homered in both wins. But the champions battled back and forced a Game 7 in Tampa Bay. Taking the mound for the Rays in the winner-take-all game was 24-year-old Matt Garza. The young righty had already won Game 3 in Boston. Now the stakes were even higher. Garza gave up a home run in the first inning. He didn't do much wrong after that. Garza gave up only one more hit before being pulled in the eighth inning. By the time he came out of the game, the Rays led 3–1.

Maddon turned to four relief pitchers to get through a tense eighth inning. The fourth was 23-year-old David Price. The left-hander had been drafted only a year earlier and made his major league debut in September 2008. But the rookie delivered. After coming on with the bases loaded, he struck out Red Sox slugger J. D. Drew. Price then struck out two more batters in the ninth as he closed out the win. The Rays were heading to the World Series in their first trip to the postseason.

They met the Philadelphia Phillies. After losing Game 1 at home, the Rays won the second game 4–2 to tie the series. But the Phillies won the next three games to win the championship. Despite the disappointing end to the playoff run, the young Rays were finally competitors.

CHAPTER 3

BETTER LATE THAN NEVER

Tampa Bay missed the playoffs in 2009 but bounced right back a year later. In 2010 the team won the AL East again. Their first playoff opponent was the Texas Rangers, who were led by former Tampa Bay draft pick Josh Hamilton. The outfielder was that year's AL MVP. After losing the first two games of the best-of-five series at home, the Rays fought back to win the next two on the road. But the Rangers won the decisive Game 5 at Tropicana Field.

Throughout the 2000s, the AL East was one of the best divisions in baseball. It continued to be tough into the 2010s. In 2011 the Yankees won the division with the best record in

Rays outfielder B. J. Upton connects during a 2011 game against the Toronto Blue Jays.

On July 26, 2010, Matt Garza threw the first no-hitter in Rays history. He walked only one batter, who was then erased on a double play, meaning Garza faced the minimum amount of 27 hitters in a 5–0 win over the Detroit Tigers. While this was the first time a Rays pitcher had thrown a no-hitter, the team was used to them in 2010. They were no-hit by Edwin Jackson of the Arizona Diamondbacks in June that season. And in May, Dallas Braden of the Oakland Athletics threw a perfect game against the Rays.

the AL. That left only a wild-card spot for either the Rays or the Boston Red Sox.

By September 3, the Rays looked to be out of the playoff race. Tampa Bay was nine games behind the Red Sox with 24 games left. But Tampa Bay got hot and won 15 out of its next 23 games. Meanwhile, the Red Sox lost 17 of 23. Entering the last day of the season, the teams had the same record. It set the stage for one of the wildest final-day finishes baseball had ever seen.

GAME 162

There was only one way the Rays could clinch a playoff spot that night. They had to win, and the Red Sox had to lose. But Tampa Bay was hosting the division-champion Yankees. The Red Sox were in Baltimore to play the Orioles, who had been in last place since the end of May. Things looked even worse for the Rays when the Yankees jumped out to a 7–0 lead. Meanwhile, the Red Sox led the Orioles 3–2.

At 9:33 p.m., a heavy rain started in Baltimore, which delayed the Red Sox–Orioles game for nearly 1 1/2 hours. During that time, the Rays started mounting a comeback. They were still down 7–0 heading into the bottom of the eighth. But Tampa Bay scratched out three runs with the help of a walk and two hit batters. It was 7–3 when Evan Longoria stepped to the plate and blasted a three-run shot to make it 7–6. That was still the score with two outs in the bottom of the ninth when lefty Dan Johnson came in to pinch hit. On a 2–2 pitch, he hit a line drive down the right-field line. It just barely stayed fair as it cleared the fence for a game-tying home run.

Dan Johnson hit just two home runs in 2011, including his dramatic game-tying shot against the New York Yankees in the ninth inning of the season's final game.

Play resumed in Baltimore at 10:58 p.m. The Orioles still trailed 3–2 with two outs in the bottom of the ninth. But three straight hits scored two runs and a walk-off win for Baltimore.

It was just past midnight in St. Petersburg when the home fans found out the Red Sox had lost. Longoria was at the plate in the bottom of the 12th facing Yankees reliever Scott Proctor. On another 2–2 pitch, Longoria hit a low line drive down the left-field line. Just like Johnson's game-tying shot, it barely cleared the fence and stayed fair. But it was enough to win the game. The rest of the Rays were waiting for him at home plate. What remained of the 30,000 fans in attendance

Evan Longoria, *right,* crosses home plate into a mob of teammates after his playoff-clinching home run on September 28, 2011.

screamed with joy. After one of baseball's most incredible final nights, the Rays were headed back to the playoffs.

Once again, Tampa Bay met the Texas Rangers in the ALDS. The series looked as though it might have a different outcome after the Rays crushed Texas 9–0 in Game 1. But the Rangers won the next three to win the series. While the playoff run was short, Tampa fans will never forget Game 162.

GAME 163

Two years later, the Rays needed more late-season heroics to reach the playoffs. After the 162-game season, the Rays and the Rangers were both 91–71 and tied for the second wild-card spot in the AL. That meant a 163rd game was needed to decide who would go to the playoffs. The Rangers had a 4–3 record against the Rays that season, so the game was played in Arlington, Texas.

Tampa Bay got on the board right away through a sacrifice fly by Delmon Young in the top of the first. Longoria added a two-run home run in the third. The Rays scored two more runs in the game, which was more than enough for Tampa Bay ace David Price. The lefty pitched a complete game in a 5–2 victory as the Rays finally got the better of Texas.

That meant the Rays had to travel to Cleveland for the AL wild-card game. Cleveland was the hottest team in baseball with 10 straight wins to finish the season. Tampa Bay's Alex Cobb stopped the streak. Cleveland got eight hits off Cobb, but the Rays' starter worked out of multiple jams to keep runs off the board. Young hit a long home run in the third inning to give the Rays the lead. Tampa Bay added three more runs to win 4–0.

Once again, Tampa Bay's playoff run ended in the ALDS. This time the Rays were beaten in four games by the division-rival Boston Red Sox. And that playoff disappointment turned out to be the end of an era.

The Rays had turned themselves into a winning team in 2008 despite having one of the lowest payrolls in the league. The days of finishing in last in the division every season were long gone. But the team struggled in 2014. With the Rays out of contention, Price was sent to the Detroit Tigers at the trade deadline in July.

More big changes came after the season. Friedman left the

PRICELESS

The Rays had a winning season in 2012, finishing 90–72. It wasn't good enough to make the playoffs, though. The silver lining of the season was the pitching of David Price. He led the AL with 20 wins and a 2.56 earned-run average (ERA). That won him the AL Cy Young Award. The award is given to the best pitcher in each league every season. Price was the first Rays pitcher ever to earn that honor.

David Price left the Rays with a team-record 3.18 career ERA.

Rays and joined the Los Angeles Dodgers. Maddon also left to take over managing the Chicago Cubs. Just like that, the Rays were starting over.

CASHING IN

After Joe Maddon left, Tampa Bay hired a manager who had never led a big-league team before. Tampa Bay native Kevin Cash took over at just 37 years old. That made him the youngest manager in the majors.

The first three seasons were a struggle for Cash. Under Sternberg, the Rays had never spent much on their roster. They continually traded away young players to avoid giving them big contracts. That included trading outfielder Wil Myers when he was 23, only one season after he won the AL Rookie of the Year.

The roster went through a major shakeup before the 2018 season. Among other moves, longtime third baseman Evan

Blake Snell set new team records with 21 wins and a 1.89 ERA in 2018.

Longoria was traded to the San Francisco Giants. The move annoyed Rays fans. Longoria had delivered many of the Rays' most memorable moments. At the time, he was considered the greatest player in team history. Longoria held many team records, including games played, home runs, runs scored, and runs batted in (RBIs).

At the trade deadline in July, the Rays were hovering around .500. But they were 20 games out of the division lead. Not feeling like they were contenders, they made more moves. One of them was sending two-time All-Star starting pitcher Chris Archer to the Pittsburgh Pirates.

Despite moving away valuable players, the Rays went on to finish the season 90–72. A big reason for this was the pitching of Blake Snell. The former first-round pick by the Rays had made his debut in 2016. After struggling early, he blossomed into a star in 2018. Just as David Price did in 2012,

THE OPENER

On May 19, 2018, the Rays used Sergio Romo as a starting pitcher. Romo had pitched in 588 games in his career, but this was his first start. The Rays wanted one of their better relievers to face the top of the Los Angeles Angels' batting order before bringing in a traditional starter to pitch most of the game. This concept became known as using an "opener" instead of a starter for a game. While the strategy was criticized by multiple teams, the Rays finished 2018 with the second-best ERA in the AL. Soon several other teams started copying the Rays' method.

Snell led the AL in wins and ERA. That earned him the AL Cy
Young Award.

TIME TO UPGRADE

After a successful 2018 season, the Rays knew they had a
chance to compete in 2019. They signed veteran starting
pitcher Charlie Morton in free agency. Morton had helped the
Houston Astros win the World Series in 2017. The late bloomer
then made his first All-Star team in 2018 at age 34. Morton
was even better in 2019 with the Rays, with career bests in
wins, strikeouts, and ERA. Morton teamed with several young
pitchers as the Rays posted the lowest ERA in the AL. Their
dominant pitching led to a 96–66 record and the team's first
playoff appearance since 2013.

The Rays had to travel to Oakland to play the Athletics in
the AL wild-card game. While pitching was the Rays' strength,
their bats came to life at the best possible time. First baseman
Yandy Díaz led off the game with a home run to right field.
He hit another solo shot in the third inning to make it 4–0.
Tampa Bay hit four home runs in the game. And Morton proved
he was worth the money on the mound. He gave up one run
in five innings of work. The bullpen shut the A's down for the
rest of the game, and the Rays moved on to the ALDS with a
5–1 victory.

Yandy Díaz connects on the first of his two home runs in the 2019 AL wild-card game.

Morton's old team, the Astros, was waiting for Tampa Bay. After the Rays lost the first two games of the series, the veteran ace got Tampa Bay on the board with a 10–3 victory in Game 3. Six different pitchers shut down Houston in Game 4. But the Astros bounced back with a 6–1 victory in the decisive fifth game. It was a fourth straight disappointing ALDS loss for Tampa Bay.

BROSSEAU'S REVENGE

The 2020 season was unlike any in baseball history. It was shortened to 60 games and played in empty stadiums due to the COVID-19 pandemic. Despite the strange circumstances, the Rays thrived. They went 40–20 and won the AL East for the first time since 2010.

The Rays swept the Toronto Blue Jays in the wild-card series, which set them up against the division-rival New York Yankees in the ALDS. The two teams had a bitter history. Since the Yankees have a spring training facility and a minor league affiliate in Tampa, there are a lot of New York fans in the area. Yankee fans flock to Tropicana Field and often outnumber Rays fans in their own stadium when the teams play there. In September 2020, Yankees closer Aroldis Chapman added more fuel to the fire. He threw a 101-mile-per-hour fastball at pinch hitter Mike Brosseau's head. The pitch just missed Brosseau, but each team's bench cleared after the game as tempers flared.

There were no intentionally hit batters during the ALDS. But it was a tense series. The teams split the first four games to set up a deciding Game 5. The game was tied 1–1 heading into the bottom of the eighth at Tropicana Field. Chapman was on the mound, and with one out, Brosseau was up to bat. Brosseau quickly went down 0–2. But he battled to make Chapman throw 10 pitches. Brosseau hammered the 10th pitch over the

Mike Brosseau, *right,* celebrates with Yandy Díaz after Brosseau's home run in the eighth inning against the Yankees in Game 5 of the 2020 ALDS.

left-field fence. That proved to be the series-winning hit. The Rays had won their first ALDS since 2008.

MORTON STRIKES BACK

That set the stage for Randy Arozarena's dramatic early home run in Game 7 against the Astros. After the blast, it was up to Morton to hold the lead. Catcher Mike Zunino drove in two more runs for the Rays in the second and sixth innings. That was more than enough run support for Morton. The ace shut down the Astros, giving up two hits and striking out six batters in over five innings of work. At one point he retired 14 straight batters. The Astros added a pair of late runs, but it wasn't enough. The Rays' 4–2 victory sent them back to the World Series for the first time in 12 years.

Righty Charlie Morton had career highs of 16 wins and 240 strikeouts for the Rays in 2019.

The Rays fell behind 2–1 in the series to the Los Angeles Dodgers. But Game 4 delivered one of the wildest finishes in recent World Series history. The Rays were down 7–6 with two outs in the bottom of the ninth of Game 4. Florida native Brett Phillips came up to the plate with runners at first and second. He singled to center to score Kevin Kiermaier from second base. But Dodgers center fielder Chris Taylor fumbled the ball. Arozarena saw that and tried to score from first. Taylor recovered the ball and fired home. Los Angeles catcher Will Smith caught the relay in plenty of time. He expected to spin and tag Arozarena, but the runner had stumbled and fallen further up the baseline. Smith didn't know that, and when he swung his glove at no one, the ball flew out. Arozarena was able to get up and dive home with the winning run.

Tampa Bay lost the next two games. Despite the World Series defeat, the Rays looked like a force again. Since he had played only part of the 2020 season, Arozarena was still considered a rookie in 2021. He proved his short 2020 season was no fluke by winning the AL Rookie of the Year. He also led the Rays to another AL East crown. Starting pitcher Shane McClanahan, who made his debut in the 2020 playoffs, and top MLB prospect Wander Franco both finished with Rookie of the Year votes as well. Rays fans hoped that the new young core could finally lead the team to its first World Series title.

Shortstop Wander Franco finished third in 2021 AL Rookie of the Year voting after hitting .288 with seven homers and 39 RBIs in just 70 games.

TIMELINE

1998

The Tampa Bay Devil Rays play their first MLB season and finish 63–99.

1999

Tampa high school product Wade Boggs collects his 3,000th hit while playing for the Devil Rays. He is the first MLB player to record hit number 3,000 on a home run.

2004

Tampa native Lou Piniella leads the Rays to a 70–91 record and their first fourth-place finish in the AL East.

2005

Tampa Bay hires Joe Maddon as its new manager in November.

2007

The team drops the word *Devil* from its name following the 2007 season.

2008

In their first season as the Rays, Tampa Bay wins the AL East for the first time and makes it to the World Series before falling 4–1 to the Philadelphia Phillies.

2010

The Rays finish with the best record in the AL and win the AL East again.

2011

Evan Longoria's 12th-inning walk-off home run against the New York Yankees caps a wild final day of the season and sends the Rays to the playoffs.

2013

The Rays reach the postseason again after winning a one-game playoff over the Texas Rangers.

2014

Joe Maddon leaves the Rays to join the Chicago Cubs. Tampa Bay hires 37-year-old Kevin Cash as his replacement.

2017

The Rays trade longtime star Evan Longoria to the San Francisco Giants.

2019

The Rays make the playoffs for the first time since 2013 and beat the Oakland A's in the AL wild-card game.

2020

Randy Arozarena sets a record for most home runs, hits, and total bases in a run to the World Series, but the Rays fall 4–2 to the Los Angeles Dodgers.

TEAM FACTS

FRANCHISE HISTORY

Tampa Bay Devil Rays
(1998–2007)
Tampa Bay Rays (2008–)

KEY PLAYERS

Chris Archer (2012–18, 2021)
Randy Arozarena (2020–)
Wade Boggs (1998–99)
Carl Crawford (2002–10)
Tyler Glasnow (2018–)
Scott Kazmir (2004–09)
Kevin Kiermaier (2013–)
Evan Longoria (2008–17)
Shane McClanahan (2020–)
Charlie Morton (2019–20)
Carlos Peña (2007–10, 2012)
David Price (2008–14)
James Shields (2006–12)
Blake Snell (2016–20)
Ben Zobrist (2006–14)

KEY MANAGERS

Kevin Cash (2015–)
Joe Maddon (2006–14)

HOME STADIUMS

Tropicana Field (1998–)

TEAM TRIVIA

TRIPLE UP

On September 2, 2006, the Rays turned the first 2-6-2 triple play in MLB history. Pitcher J. P. Howell struck out Raúl Ibañez of the Seattle Mariners with runners on first and third. Catcher Dioner Navarro threw to shortstop Ben Zobrist for the second out. Zobrist then returned the ball home to retire the runner breaking for the plate.

TOUCH TANK

Since 2006 Tropicana Field has featured the Rays Touch Experience. The exhibit is a giant water tank where fans can touch stingrays as they swim.

MAKING HISTORY

On September 15, 2022, the Rays became the first team to start an all-Latino batting order. Tampa Bay's lineup included three players from the Dominican Republic, two from Venezuela, two from Cuba, one from Colombia, and one from Mexico.

ON THE CATWALK

There are four catwalks suspended from the ceiling in fair territory at Tropicana Field. If a ball strikes either of the two lower catwalks, it is ruled a home run. If it hits one of the upper catwalks, it can bounce back into play. Fielders can even catch it for an out. Any ball that lands on a catwalk and stays there is ruled a double.

GLOSSARY

bullpen

The area on a baseball field where relief pitchers can warm up; also used to refer to a team's relievers as a group.

debut

First appearance.

free agency

A period of time in the offseason during which players who don't have a current contract can sign with any team.

investor

A person who puts money into financial plans expecting to make a profit.

no-hitter

A game in which a pitcher doesn't allow any hits.

payroll

The amount of money a team spends on its roster.

perfect game

A game in which a pitcher doesn't allow any batters to reach base.

spring training

The preseason, which takes place in February and March in Florida and Arizona.

walk-off

When the home team wins by taking the lead in the bottom of the ninth or in extra innings.

wild card

A team that doesn't win its division but still makes the playoffs.

MORE INFORMATION

BOOKS

Flynn, Brendan. *The MLB Encyclopedia*. Minneapolis, MN: Abdo Publishing, 2022.

Gitlin, Marty. *Baseball Underdog Stories*. Minneapolis, MN: Abdo Publishing, 2019.

Hewson, Anthony K. *GOATs of Baseball*. Minneapolis, MN: Abdo Publishing, 2022.

ONLINE RESOURCES

To learn more about the Tampa Bay Rays, please visit **abdobooklinks.com** or scan this QR code. These links are routinely monitored and updated to provide the most current information available.

INDEX

Abreu, Bobby, 10
Archer, Chris, 34
Arozarena, Randy, 6–7, 38, 40

Baldelli, Rocco, 16–17
Boggs, Wade, 10, 13
Braden, Dallas, 26
Brosseau, Mike, 37

Cash, Kevin, 33
Chapman, Aroldis, 37
Cobb, Alex, 30
Crawford, Carl, 17–19

Díaz, Yandy, 35
DiMaggio, Joe, 17

Franco, Wander, 40
Friedman, Andrew, 18, 30

Garza, Matt, 23, 26
Gooden, Dwight, 10

Hamilton, Josh, 15, 25
Haynes, Nathan, 19

Jackson, Edwin, 26
Johnson, Dan, 27–28

Kazmir, Scott, 18
Kiermaier, Kevin, 40

Lake, Jack, 7–8
Longoria, Evan, 7, 21, 23, 27–29, 33–34

Maddon, Joe, 18, 23, 31, 33
Margot, Manuel, 6
Martinez, Tino, 10
McClanahan, Shane, 40
McGriff, Fred, 10
Morris, Jim, 15
Morton, Charlie, 35–36, 38
Myers, Wil, 33

Naimoli, Vince, 8–9, 15, 17

Peña, Carlos, 21
Perez, Fernando, 21

Phillips, Brett, 40
Piniella, Lou, 17
Price, David, 23, 29–30, 34

Romo, Sergio, 34

Saunders, Tony, 9–10
Sternberg, Stuart, 17–18
Stocker, Kevin, 10

Upton, B. J., 18, 21

Vaughn, Greg, 15

Young, Delmon, 18, 29–30

Zunino, Mike, 38

ABOUT THE AUTHOR

Luke Hanlon is a sportswriter and editor based in Minneapolis. He grew up in the suburbs of Chicago and enjoyed many trips to Wrigley Field.